Shopping
in pictures

**Pictures
to share**

for Michelle,
one of Britain's
best shoppers.

**Pictures
to share**

First published in 2009 by
Pictures to Share Community Interest Company,
a UK based social enterprise that publishes
illustrated books for older people.

www.picturestoshare.co.uk

ISBN 978-0-9553940-9-6

Shopping
in pictures

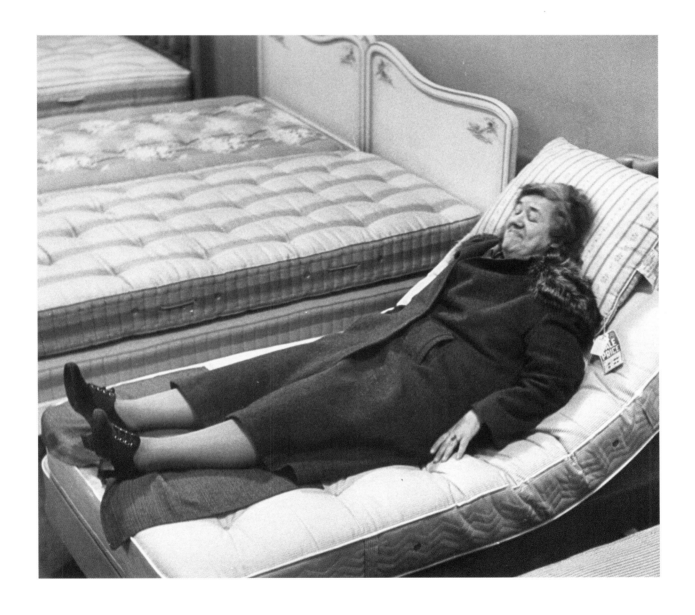

Edited by Helen J Bate

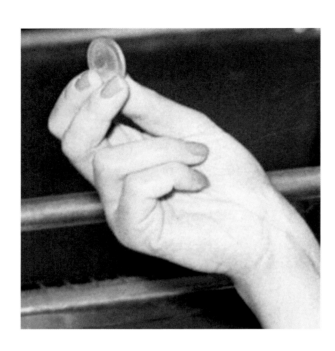

Fares please...

Watching the world go by,

Under a sunny sky,
Oh how the moments fly,
Watching the world go by.

Painting: La Place Pigalle, Paris, 1880s (oil on canvas),
by Pierre Carriere-Belleuse/Pushkin Museum, Moscow,
Russia/Bridgeman Art Library/Getty Images

Quotation: Song title. sung by Dean Martin

6

Pierre Carrier-Belleuse

I've got sixpence,

Jolly, jolly sixpence

I've got sixpence to last me all my life.

Market Scene
(oil on canvas)

by Henry C. Bryant
(1835 - 1915)

Henry Bryant was a popular painter specialising in farmyard and market scenes which were noted for their great attention to detail.

Can I help you?

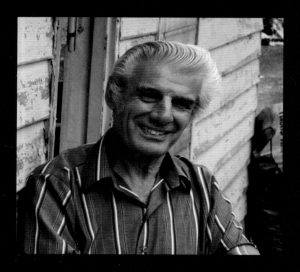

I've been a hairdresser all my life.

This wooden hut has been here for seventy-five years.

I'm a Cypriot. I was in the army, then I came to England in 1947 just after the war.

I worked on the American bases for nineteen years as a hairdresser.

I could
have danced
all night

Photograph: A teenager tries on a long evening dress in the Junior Miss
department of a large store. © Bert Hardy/Hulton Archive/Getty Images

Quotation: Song from the musical 'My Fair Lady' with lyrics by Alan Jay Lerner

Your first car?

18

Happiness

lies not in the
mere possession of money;
it lies in the enjoyment
of achievement,
in the thrill of creative effort

If you have
two loaves of bread,

sell one
and buy a lily.

I get plenty of time to think sitting here.

Not a day goes by that somebody doesn't come in and talk over their problems.

Photographs: Basket Maker 1982, Oliver Meek, age 86, Station Street, Swaffham, Norfolk. © John Londei/Dewi Lewis. Publishing 2007

Quotation: Oliver Meek From Shutting up Shop by John Londei

I learned what is
obvious to a child.

That each day should be spent
finding beauty in flowers and poetry
and talking to animals.

Photograph: A little girl is selling the first primroses of the season
at her garden gate. © Fox Photo's/Hulton Archive/Getty images

Quotation: Nicholas Sparks American Author and Writer, b.1965.
http://thinkexist.com

Anyone who keeps
the ability to see beauty
never grows old

Painting: In the Souk, by Moritz Stifter (1857-1905). Berko Fine Paintings, Knokke-Zoute, Belgium/The Bridgeman Art LIbrary/Getty Images

Quotation: Franz Kafka, German Writer 1883-1924 http://thinkexist.com

How much is that doggy in the window?

Photographs: Woman Window Shopping with Fox Terrier
by Cecil Beaton 1932 © Condé Nast Archive/CORBIS

Quotation: from song 'How much is that doggy in the window'
a popular novelty song written by Bob Merrill in 1952.

Shopping
for a television
in the 1950's

Photograph: Window shopping in
the Scottish industrial town of
Kilmarnock. © Malcolm Dunbar/Hulton
Archive/Getty Images

The easiest way
for your children
to learn about money,
is for you not to have any.

Oh! Bury me in books when I am dead,
Fair quarto leaves of ivory and gold,
And silk octavos, bound in brown and red,
That tales of love and chivalry unfold.

The way you wear your hat

The way you sip your tea,

The memory of all that
No, they can't take that
away from me

Photograph: Seed merchant 1986. F.A Bone, High Street, Rickmansworth, Hertfordshire.
© John Londei/Dewi Lewis Publishing 2007

Only tobacco. I sell tobacco, nothing else!

Not even chewing gum.

Every morning I get up at 5.20
and open the shop at 7 o'clock.

I shut at five in the evening.

We always make sure we are in bed by 9.30

Photograph (facing page): Tobacconist, Tom Cornish, Clerkenwell Road, London.
1974 © John Londei/Dewi Lewis Publishing

Quotation: William Hadley (on right in photograph), proprieter. From Shutting
up Shop by John Londei published by Dewi Lewis Publishing 2007

Tell me,
What do you get
At the end of the day?

Main photograph: A boy gives a dog a lift in his bicycle basket.
Reg Speller/Hulton Archive/Getty Images

Quotation: from the song 'At The End of The Day' by Van Morrison,
Irish singer and songwriter born 1945

**Pictures
to share**

Acknowledgements

Our thanks to the many contributors who have allowed their text or imagery to be used for a reduced or no fee.

All effort has been made to contact copyright holders. If you own the copyright for work that is represented, but have not been contacted, please get in touch via our website.

Thanks to our sponsors

ANDREWS CHARITABLE TRUST

Published by

Pictures to Share Community Interest Company.
Tattenhall, Cheshire

www.picturestoshare.co.uk

Graphics by Duncan Watts
Printed in Europe

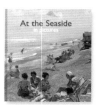

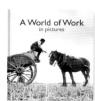

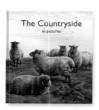

To see our other titles go to
www.picturestoshare.co.uk